The
AMERICAN
HERITAGE
dic·tion·ar·y

Define·a·Thon™

FOR

KIDS

THE NEW WORD GAME
SENSATION

Houghton Mifflin
BOSTON · NEW YORK

Visit our websites: www.ahdictionary.com *or*
www.houghtonmifflinbooks.com

Library of Congress Cataloging-in-Publication Data

The American Heritage dictionary define-a-thon for kids : the new word
game sensation.
    p. cm.
  ISBN-13: 978-0-547-02677-0 (alk. paper)
  ISBN-10: 0-547-02677-3 (alk. paper)
  1. Vocabulary--Juvenile literature. 2. Word games--Juvenile literature. 3.
Educational games--Juvenile literature. I. Houghton Mifflin Company. II.
Title: Define-a-thon for kids.
  PE1449.A4625 2008
  428.1--dc22

                                                          2007045114

Text design by Anne Chalmers

Manufactured in the United States of America

EB 10 9 8 7 6 5 4 3 2 1

Contents

Define-α-Thon
Word Challenge

Define-α-Thon
Word Challenge
R E V E A L E D

Define-α-Thon
Answer Key

Preface

Welcome to the American Heritage Define-a-Thon challenge!

The Define-a-Thon challenge dares you to test your knowledge of words by playing a quiz. The quiz questions consist of a definition along with four words that might fit the definition. But only one word is correct! The other words often sound or look like the correct word, so you have to think a little before you choose.

The quiz questions are presented all together in the first part of the book. The answers are given in the second part. Not only do you learn what the correct answers are, you also learn what the wrong answers mean. In this way you can learn more words no matter what.

The second part of the book also tells you more about the correct answer words. You can see how they are used correctly in sentences. For many words you can see how they have been used in books that kids often read in school. These books are all-time favorites like *A Wrinkle in Time*, *The Hobbit*, and *Harriet the Spy*.

Most words have interesting stories behind them, stories of where they came from and what they used to mean long ago. You can learn about the background of words in short sections called etymologies. These appear in brackets just below the example sentences. For some words you can also

---

read about the word's past in more detail in a note.

The American Heritage editors hope that you have fun learning about words in this book. They also hope that you will challenge your friends and family as well by asking them the quiz questions. That way, you will remember the answers better and look even smarter.

— Joe Pickett
Executive Editor

— Steve Kleinedler
Supervising Editor

Guide to the Define-a-Thon

The first part of the book, the Define-a-Thon Word Challenge, consists of a series of definitions. Each definition is followed by four possible answers. Only one of these answers is correct. It is your job to figure out the correct answer.

The second part, the Define-a-Thon Word Challenge Revealed, is much more than an answer key. It gives you different kinds of information about the words used in the Define-a-Thon. We tell you what each answer word means (whether it is the correct answer or not). That way, you can see how all the words differ.

We also show how the correct answer words are used properly in a sentence. For some words we show how they have been used by famous writers that kids like to read or are assigned to read in school.

We also explain where the correct answer words came from. This information, appearing between square brackets, is called the *etymology*. It tells you what language the word came from, how the word entered the English language, and sometimes how the word is related to other words.

For example, many English words are taken from Latin or Greek, especially as these languages were used in ancient times. Other words were borrowed from modern foreign languages or from languages as they were used during medieval times, especially French or the language called *Norse* (spoken by the Vikings and other Scandinavians). For some words we tell the story of how the word entered into English in greater detail in a special note.

Following the Define-a-Thon Word Challenge Revealed is a simple answer key that lists the correct answers at a glance, so you can remind yourself quickly and not forget.

Define-a-Thon
Word Challenge

1. To make up and perform without planning beforehand.

advise   improvise

revise   supervise

2. An area of flat land that is higher than the land around it.

isthmus   meadow

plateau   ripple

3. Relating to or affecting the whole world; worldwide.

harrowing   literal

obscure   universal

4. Not willing to work or be active; tending to do very little.

busy   cloudy

lazy   noisy

5. To fit in or combine with something else in a pleasant or appealing way.

fossilize   harmonize

hypnotize   realize

6. Small and unimportant; trivial.

      jetty   petty

      putty   witty

7. To make a series of high chirping sounds.

      flutter   mutter

      stutter   twitter

8. One of the pair of thin, movable organs on the heads of insects, used for touching and smelling.

      ankle   antenna

      anther   antler

9. Having a hidden or mysterious meaning.

      chaotic   cryptic

      drastic   hectic

10. A river or stream that flows into a larger river or stream.

      gulf   peninsula

     tributary   whirlpool

11. A figure in Egyptian mythology with the body of a lion and the head of a man, ram, or hawk.

centaur   lynx

mummy   sphinx

12. Required by a set of rules or the people in charge.

impartial   mandatory

mutual   optional

13. To criticize for a fault in a gentle but serious way.

admonish   astonish

relinquish   relish

14. Completely different from another thing or person.

adjacent   extinct

opposite   similar

15. An animal, such as a dog, mouse, or horse, having four feet.

quadruped   quarter

quartet   quartz

16. The ability to fight off a disease and stay healthy.

agility   anger

immunity   intelligence

17. Excused from a duty or rule that is supposed to apply to everyone in a group.

excessive   exclusive

exempt   explicit

18. A state of being peaceful or calm.

adversity   futility

humidity   serenity

19. A water-filled container for keeping and displaying fish or other water animals and often water plants.

aquarium   cranium

podium   terrarium

20. Not letting light pass through.

luminous   opaque

transatlantic   transparent

21. Harmful if swallowed, breathed in, or allowed to get on the skin; poisonous.

antique harsh

nasty toxic

22. The science, activity, and business of growing crops and raising livestock; farming.

agriculture architecture

legislature overture

23. Mysterious and strange.

uncanny unkempt

unruly unsightly

24. To supply with water by means of a system of ditches, pipes, and canals.

fertilize irrigate

marinate precipitate

25. To put into or express in another language.

annihilate edit

identify translate

26. The scientific study of the origin, history, and structure of the earth.

archaeology   biology

geology   psychology

27. A place where a large amount of water has been collected and stored for use.

dromedary   granary

reservoir   warehouse

28. A chemical element that is a silvery-white, radioactive metal. It is heavy and poisonous and is used for fuel in nuclear reactors.

aluminum   oxygen

sodium   uranium

29. The gas that surrounds a body in space, especially the air that surrounds the earth.

atmosphere   cashmere

gondolier   hemisphere

30. To influence or manage in a clever or sneaky way.

agitate   cultivate

dispel   manipulate

31. To walk slowly and with effort; plod.

    dwell   hover

    traipse   trudge

32. Peaceful and quiet.

    dubious   grim

    insolent   tranquil

33. Dull because of always being the same.

    anonymous   delirious

    monotonous   notorious

34. The distance around the outside of something, such as a space or geometric figure.

    diameter   perimeter

    radius   volume

35. An automatic response by a living thing to something else.

    annex   apex

    index   reflex

36. Friendly and pleasant; good-natured.

adventurous   advisable

amiable   applicable

37. The freight carried by a ship, airplane, or other large vehicle.

cargo   embargo

lingo   logo

38. Fresh and clean; not spoiled or decayed.

boisterous   listless

pessimistic   pristine

39. A covering of waterproof canvas used to protect something outdoors.

duct   enclosure

tarpaulin   trampoline

40. The total number of people living in a certain place.

accumulation   circulation

identification   population

41. Not making any sense; silly.

absurd   jovial

pertinent   solemn

42. Typical of cats.

bovine   canine

equine   feline

43. A view of everything that can be seen over a wide area.

panorama   porthole

silhouette   spectacle

44. A lifting or upward movement of the earth's crust.

acceleration   instep

upheaval   valley

45. To bend or hang downward.

drain   dread

drizzle   droop

46. To carry from one place to another.

import report

support transport

47. A positive or negative whole number or zero.

fraction infinity

integer ratio

48. Eating many kinds of food, including both meat and plants.

carnivorous omnivorous

ravenous venomous

49. A weight hung, as in a clock, so that it can swing back and forth.

equilibrium fulcrum

pendulum spectrum

50. A person riding in a car, airplane, or other vehicle.

participant passenger

pedestrian spectator

51. Needing immediate attention.

> current   impressive
>
> trite   urgent

52. With the hands on the hips and the elbows bent outward.

> akimbo   combo
>
> hobo   jumbo

53. Easily harmed or attacked.

> abominable   durable
>
> tolerable   vulnerable

54. Following one right after the other.

> affirmative   consecutive
>
> defective   diminutive

55. To cover, surround, or line with a material that slows or prevents heat, electricity, or sound from passing through.

> gorge   insulate
>
> lubricate   upholster

56. A word or phrase used by a business, team, or other group to advertise its aims or beliefs.

mascot   notation

refrain   slogan

57. To prevent from doing something; hold back.

relieve   repeal

restrain   retire

58. A small guitar with four strings.

accordion   harp

ukulele   xylophone

Define-a-Thon
Word Challenge
REVEALED

As time dragged on, she sang to pass the hours. At first she invented rhymes about the tundra and sang them to tunes she had learned at school. When she tired of these melodies she **improvised** on the songs of her childhood.

—Jean Craighead George
Julie of the Wolves

1.

improvise

To make up and perform without planning beforehand.

The candidate had forgotten her notes, so she improvised a speech on the spot.

[From the Italian word *improvviso*, "unforeseen."]

WHAT THE OTHER WORDS MEAN

advise: To give or offer advice to someone.

revise: To change or make different.

supervise: To watch over and inspect the action or work of someone.

plateau

An area of flat land that is higher than the land around it.

After they climbed up to the plateau, they could see for miles in all directions.

[From the French word *plateau*, "plateau," which is related to the French word *plat*, "flat."]

WHAT THE OTHER WORDS MEAN

isthmus: A narrow strip of land with water on both sides, connecting two larger masses of land.

meadow: An area of grassy ground, such as one used as a pasture.

ripple: A small wave that forms when the surface of water is disturbed.

3.

universal

Relating to or affecting the whole world; worldwide.

A large increase in the price of oil would have a universal effect on trade.

[From the Latin word *universum,* "universe."]

WHAT THE OTHER WORDS MEAN

harrowing: Causing great distress; agonizing.

literal: Following the usual or exact meaning of a word or group of words.

obscure: Not well known.

4.

lazy

Not willing to work or be active;
tending to do very little.

*Lazy students usually get
poor grades.*

[Perhaps related to the medieval Norse word
lasinn, "broken-down, ill, sick."]

WHAT THE OTHER WORDS MEAN

busy: Engaged in work or activity.

cloudy: Full of or covered with
clouds.

noisy: Making a lot of noise; very
loud.

5.

harmonize

To fit in or combine with something else in a pleasant or appealing way.

In our school's choir, the voices of the sopranos harmonize well with the voices of the tenors.

[Ultimately from the Greek word *harmonia*, "agreement, harmony."]

WHAT THE OTHER WORDS MEAN

fossilize: To change the remains of a plant or animal into a fossil by trapping them in rock or other material and preserving them over time.

hypnotize: To put into a relaxed, sleep-like, but alert state.

realize: To become fully aware of something; understand something clearly.

6.

petty

Small and unimportant; trivial.

*He kept bothering the
waiter with petty requests.*

[From the French word *petit*, "small."]

WHAT THE OTHER WORDS MEAN

jetty: A structure, such as a pier, that is built out into a body of water to protect a harbor or shoreline from strong waves.

putty: A doughlike substance that is used to fill holes and seal cracks.

witty: Clever and funny.

And all of a sudden I saw that if life seems awfully petty most of the time, every now and then there is something noble and beautiful and almost pure that lifts us suddenly out of the **pettiness** and lets us share in it a little.

—Laurence Yep
Dragonwings

7.

twitter

To make a series of high chirping sounds.

*The baby birds are twitter-
ing in the nest.*

[From the medieval English word *twiteren*, "to
chirp." The sound of the word *twiteren* is
meant to imitate chirping birds.]

WHAT THE OTHER WORDS MEAN

flutter: To flap rapidly like the
wings of a bird.

mutter: To speak in low sounds that
are difficult to understand.

stutter: To speak with many short
pauses and repetitions of
sounds.

8.

antenna

One of the pair of thin, movable organs on the heads of insects, used for touching and smelling.

The two ants are communicating by touching each other's antennas.

[From the Latin word *antenna*, "a type of horizontal pole to which a ship's sails are attached." Medieval scientists later used this word to describe insect antennas, since they stick out like these poles.]

WHAT THE OTHER WORDS MEAN

ankle: The joint between the foot and the leg.

anther: The part of the flower that produces and contains pollen.

antler: A bony growth on the head of some animals, such as deer and antelopes.

9.

cryptic

Having a hidden or mysterious meaning.

We could not understand his cryptic hand signals, so we could not do what he wanted until he explained what he meant.

[From the Greek word *kruptein*, "to hide."]

WHAT THE OTHER WORDS MEAN

chaotic: In great disorder or confusion.

drastic: Extreme or severe in effect.

hectic: Full of activity, confusion, or excitement.

tributary

A river or stream that flows into a larger river or stream.

We canoed down the tributary into the river.

[From the Latin word *tributum*, "contribution."]

WHAT THE OTHER WORDS MEAN

gulf: A large area of a sea or ocean that is partly enclosed by land.

peninsula: A piece of land that sticks out into water from a larger land mass.

whirlpool: A current of water that rotates very rapidly.

11.

sphinx

A figure in Egyptian mythology with the body of a lion and the head of a man, ram, or hawk.

The Great Sphinx of Egypt is a stone lion with a human head and paws that are fifty feet long.

[From the Greek word *sphinx.*]

WHAT THE OTHER WORDS MEAN

centaur: A creature in Greek mythology that has the head, arms, and chest of a human and the body and legs of a horse.

lynx: A wild cat with thick, soft fur, tufts of hair on its ears, and a short tail.

mummy: The body of a person that has been specially treated after death to preserve it from decay.

The English word **sphinx** comes from the Greek language. To the Greeks, the most famous sphinx was not the Great Sphinx of Egypt near the pyramids. It was a legendary monster that lived near Thebes, a Greek city. This sphinx killed anyone who could not answer the following riddle: "What has two feet, and four feet, and three feet, and is slowest when it goes on four feet?" The sphinx killed itself when the hero Oedipus gave this answer: "A human being, who crawls as a baby, walks upright as an adult, and uses a cane when old."

The ultimate origin of the Greek word *sphinx* is still an unsolved riddle. Some modern experts think that Greek *sphinx* comes from the Egyptian word *shezep-ankh,* meaning "living image" and "statue." *Shezep* means "image," while *ankh* means "life."

The hieroglyphic symbol for *ankh,* "life," is a cross with a loop at the top. In modern times, the *ankh* symbol is often used as a pendant on necklaces.

mandatory

Required by a set of rules or the people in charge.

It is mandatory for all restaurant workers to wash their hands before serving food.

[From the Latin word *mandatum*, "order, command."]

WHAT THE OTHER WORDS MEAN

impartial: Not favoring either side.

mutual: Having the same relationship to each other.

optional: Not required.

13.

admonish

To criticize for a fault in a gentle but serious way.

*The coach admonished me
for skipping soccer practice.*

[From the Latin word *admonere*, "to remind, to admonish."]

WHAT THE OTHER WORDS MEAN

astonish: To surprise greatly; amaze.

relinquish: To give up or let go of something.

relish: To get pleasure from something; enjoy.

opposite

Completely different from another thing or person.

I'm short and talkative, and my sister's the opposite— tall and quiet.

[From the Latin word *oppositus,* "opposed, opposite."]

WHAT THE OTHER WORDS MEAN

adjacent: Next to or close to something or someone.

extinct: No longer existing in living form.

similar: Alike but not exactly the same.

15.

quadruped

An animal, such as a dog, mouse, or horse, having four feet.

Scientists believe that the ancestor of snakes was a quadruped.

[From the Latin word *quadrupes*, "four-footed," made up of the Latin words *quattuor*, "four," and *pes*, "foot."]

WHAT THE OTHER WORDS MEAN

quarter: Any of four equal parts into which something can be divided.

quartet: A group of four people or four things.

quartz: A clear, hard mineral that is found in rocks.

16.

immunity

The ability to fight off a disease and stay healthy.

The measles vaccine gives you immunity, so you will not get the disease even if you are around people who have it.

[From the Latin word *immunis*, "free from a duty or burden."]

WHAT THE OTHER WORDS MEAN

agility: Quickness and ease in moving or thinking.

anger: A strong feeling of not being pleased with someone or something.

intelligence: The ability to learn, think, understand, and know.

exempt

Excused from a duty or rule that is supposed to apply to everyone in a group.

You are exempt from wash-ing the dishes while you have a cast on your arm.

[From the Latin word *exemptus*, "taken out, exempt."]

WHAT THE OTHER WORDS MEAN

excessive: Greater than is normal, proper, or necessary.

exclusive: Not shared with others; sole.

explicit: Clearly stated so that noth-ing is misunderstood.

Surely her mother must know what people were saying, must be aware of the smugly vicious gossip. Surely it must hurt her as it did Meg. But if it did she gave no outward sign. Nothing ruffled the **serenity** of her expression.

—Madeleine L'Engle
A Wrinkle in Time

18.

serenity

A state of being peaceful or calm.

We enjoyed the serenity of the quiet evening after the violent afternoon thunderstorms.

[From the Latin word *serenus*, "clear, serene."]

WHAT THE OTHER WORDS MEAN

adversity: Great misfortune; hardship.

futility: The condition of having no useful result; uselessness.

humidity: Moisture in the air.

19.

aquarium

A water-filled container for keeping and displaying fish or other water animals and often water plants.

She keeps several types of fish and some snails in her aquarium.

[From the Latin word *aqua*, "water."]

WHAT THE OTHER WORDS MEAN

cranium: The part of the skull that encloses the brain.

podium: An elevated platform, such as one used by the conductor of an orchestra or someone giving a lecture.

terrarium: A closed container for keeping and displaying small land plants and sometimes land animals, such as turtles and lizards.

opaque

Not letting light pass through.

He hung opaque curtains in the bedroom so the sun would not wake him up early in the morning.

[From the Latin word *opacus*, "dark, shady."]

WHAT THE OTHER WORDS MEAN

luminous: Giving off light; shining.

transatlantic: Spanning or crossing the Atlantic Ocean.

transparent: Allowing light to pass through so that objects on the other side can be seen clearly.

toxic

Harmful if swallowed, breathed in, or allowed to get on the skin; poisonous.

Those berries are toxic; don't let the dog eat them.

[From the Greek word *toxikon*, "poison for arrows."]

WHAT THE OTHER WORDS MEAN

antique: Made at a time many years in the past.

harsh: Unpleasant to hear or taste.

nasty: Dirty, disgusting, or offensive.

22.

agriculture

The science, activity, and business of growing crops and raising livestock; farming.

Agriculture declined in the region when many farmers began to move to the city.

[From the Latin word *agricultura*, "agriculture," from *ager*, "field."]

WHAT THE OTHER WORDS MEAN

architecture: The art of designing buildings.

legislature: A body of people with the power to make and change laws.

overture: A musical work that is played by an orchestra before a larger work, such as an opera or ballet.

23.

uncanny

Mysterious and strange.

It's uncanny the way our dog goes to sit by the door ten minutes before my father arrives home.

[*Uncanny* was made by adding the prefix *un-*, "not," to the Scottish word *canny,* "lucky, safe, cozy."]

WHAT THE OTHER WORDS MEAN

unkempt: Not neat or tidy; messy.

unruly: Hard to control or keep in order.

unsightly: Not pleasant to look at; ugly.

The nights were comfortless and chill, and they did not dare to sing or talk too loud, for the echoes were **uncanny**, and the silence seemed to dislike being broken—except by the noise of water and the wail of wind and the crack of stone.

—J.R.R. Tolkien
The Hobbit

irrigate

To supply with water by means of a system of ditches, pipes, and canals.

In this dry climate, orchards have to be irrigated.

[From the Latin word *irrigare*, "to water, to irrigate."]

WHAT THE OTHER WORDS MEAN

fertilize: To add manure or chemicals to soil so that grass and plants will grow better.

marinate: To soak meat or fish in a liquid mixture before cooking.

precipitate: To change from vapor to water and fall as rain, snow, sleet, or hail.

translate

To put into or express in another language.

The best-selling novel was translated into Arabic, Chinese, and ten other languages.

[From the Latin word *translatus*, "brought over."]

WHAT THE OTHER WORDS MEAN

annihilate: To destroy completely.

edit: To correct or revise something that is written, such as a report or a letter.

identify: To recognize and acknowledge who someone is or what something is.

geology

The scientific study of the origin, history, and structure of the earth.

In geology class we learned why there are more earthquakes in Alaska and California than in other parts of the United States.

[Ultimately from the Greek word *ge*, "earth," added to the English suffix *-logy*, "study of."]

WHAT THE OTHER WORDS MEAN

archaeology: The scientific study of past human culture as it is shown by the tools, pottery, and other items from past societies.

biology: The scientific study of living things and life processes.

psychology: The scientific study of the mind, the emotions, and human behavior.

reservoir

A place where a large amount of water has been collected and stored for use.

You aren't allowed to swim in the reservoir because drinking water for the city is drawn from there.

[From the French word *réservoir,* from *réserver,* to reserve.]

WHAT THE OTHER WORDS MEAN

dromedary: A camel with one hump.

granary: A building for storing grain.

warehouse: A large building where merchandise is stored.

uranium

A chemical element that is a silvery-white, radioactive metal. It is heavy and poisonous and is used for fuel in nuclear reactors.

When a uranium atom is split, energy is produced.

[Uranium was named after the planet Uranus.]

WHAT THE OTHER WORDS MEAN

aluminum: A chemical element that is a lightweight, silvery-white metal. Aluminum can easily be made into different shapes and is a good conductor of electricity.

oxygen: A chemical element that is a colorless, odorless gas. Oxygen makes up about one-fifth of the earth's atmosphere. Animals need oxygen to live.

sodium: A chemical element that is a soft, lightweight, silvery-white metal. Sodium combines with chlorine to make the salt that is used to season food.

Uranium owes its name to the planet Uranus. In 1781, the British astronomer Sir William Herschel discovered a new planet beyond Saturn. He wanted to name the planet after George III, the king of England. French astronomers wanted to call it Herschel. Eventually, it was named Uranus, after the Greek and Roman god of the sky.

In Greek and Roman mythology, the god Mars is the son of the god Jupiter. Jupiter himself is the son of the god Saturn. In this way, starting at the sun and moving outwards, the order of the planets Mars, Jupiter, and Saturn shows the family relationships among the gods. Astronomers decided to continue this pattern. They named the next planet beyond Saturn after the god Uranus, who was Saturn's father and Jupiter's grandfather.

A few years later, in 1789, the German chemist Martin Heinrich Klaproth discovered a new element. He named it uranium to honor the discovery of Uranus.

atmosphere

The gas that surrounds a body in space, especially the air that surrounds the earth.

The atmosphere of the planet Venus is composed mainly of carbon dioxide.

[From the Greek words *atmos*, "vapor," and *sphaira*, "ball, sphere."]

WHAT THE OTHER WORDS MEAN

cashmere: The fine, soft wool of an Asian goat.

gondolier: The person who rows a gondola, usually with a single oar.

hemisphere: One half of a sphere.

manipulate

To influence or manage in a clever or sneaky way.

He was always able to manipulate his friends into doing what he wanted to do.

[From English *manipulation*, "skillful operation," ultimately from Spanish *manipulación*, originally meaning "use of chemicals in experiments," from Latin *manipulus*, "handful."]

WHAT THE OTHER WORDS MEAN

agitate: To upset the mind or feelings of someone; disturb.

cultivate: To grow or tend a crop or a field.

dispel: To rid one's mind of something.

31.

trudge

To walk slowly and with effort; plod.

She trudged up the steep mountain trail with her heavy backpack.

[The origin of the word *trudge* is unknown. The first known appearance of *trudge* in writing dates from 1547.]

WHAT THE OTHER WORDS MEAN

dwell: To live as a resident somewhere; reside.

hover: To remain in one place in the air.

traipse: To walk or wander about.

tranquil

Peaceful and quiet.

They walked by the tranquil lake in the evening, looking at the reflection of the moon on its calm surface.

[From the Latin word *tranquillus*, "tranquil."]

WHAT THE OTHER WORDS MEAN

dubious: Feeling or showing doubt.

grim: Not pleasant or favorable; gloomy.

insolent: Disrespectful of people in authority; rude.

Clicketta, clicketta, clicketta. The song of the locomotive was **monotonous** as they traveled north, and the hours seemed like Mama's never-ending ball of thread unwinding in front of them.

—Pam Muñoz Ryan
Esperanza Rising

monotonous

Dull because of always being the same.

At first she liked wearing a uniform to school, but after a few weeks it began to seem monotonous.

[From the Greek words *monos,* "single," and *tonos,* "tone."]

WHAT THE OTHER WORDS MEAN

anonymous: By or from someone whose name is not known or not given.

delirious: Extremely confused, especially because of being sick.

notorious: Well known for something bad or unpleasant.

perimeter

The distance around the outside of something, such as a space or geometric figure.

The swimming pool is fifteen feet wide and thirty feet long, so the perimeter is ninety feet.

[From the Greek word *perimetros*, "circumference."]

WHAT THE OTHER WORDS MEAN

diameter: The width of a circle.

radius: The distance from the outside of a circle to its center.

volume: The amount of space that something takes up.

reflex

An automatic response by a living thing to something else.

*Pulling your hand away
from a burning-hot surface
is a reflex.*

[From the Latin word *reflexus*, "the act of bending back."]

WHAT THE OTHER WORDS MEAN

annex: To add or attach.

apex: The peak or highest point of something.

index: An alphabetized list of the names and subjects in a book, giving the page or pages where each can be found.

36.

amiable

Friendly and pleasant; good-natured.

We enjoy Rosa's company because she is so amiable.

[From the French word *amiable*, "amiable," which comes from the Latin word *amicus*, "friend."]

WHAT THE OTHER WORDS MEAN

adventurous: Willing to risk danger in order to have exciting experiences.

advisable: Wise or sensible to do.

applicable: Capable of being applied to the matter at hand; relevant or appropriate.

cargo

The freight carried by a ship, air-plane, or other large vehicle.

The ship was loaded with coffee beans, bananas, and other cargo.

[From the Spanish word *carga*, "load, cargo."]

WHAT THE OTHER WORDS MEAN

embargo: An order by a government that prevents people from buying products that come from a particular country.

lingo: The special vocabulary used by a particular group of people, such as police officers or computer programmers.

logo: A symbol or design that identifies a product or business.

38.

pristine

Fresh and clean; not spoiled or decayed.

Scientists worked to keep the pristine lake free of toxic waste.

[From the Latin word *pristinus*, "pristine."]

WHAT THE OTHER WORDS MEAN

boisterous: Loud, noisy, and unruly.

listless: Too tired or too weak to want to do anything.

pessimistic: Tending to take the gloomiest or least hopeful view of a situation.

It turned out that the *Britannic* was in even better shape than I'd dared hope. Yes, she was encrusted with a thin layer of barnacles and coral, but the hull and upper decks were amazingly well preserved. The outer covering that protected the dome over the grand staircase remained intact—most of the panes of glass were still in place! The railings and items of deck hardware looked only in need of a wire brush to return them to an almost **pristine** state.

—Robert D. Ballard
Ghost Liners

tarpaulin

A covering of waterproof canvas used to protect something outdoors.

The workers put a tarpaulin over the roof they were repairing when they finished for the day.

[*Tarpaulin* probably comes from the English words *tar* and *pall*, "a piece of fabric," since tar is used to waterproof fabric.]

WHAT THE OTHER WORDS MEAN

duct: A tube or passage through which a liquid or gas flows.

enclosure: An area that is surrounded by a fence or wall.

trampoline: A strong, taut sheet, usually made of canvas, attached with springs to a metal frame and used for bouncing and performing tricks.

population

The total number of people living in a certain place.

The population of the state is increasing because many people are moving there to retire.

[From the Latin word *populus*, "people."]

WHAT THE OTHER WORDS MEAN

accumulation: An amount that has piled up, come together, or gotten bigger.

circulation: The number of copies of something, such as a newspaper, that are sold to the public.

identification: Something that is used to prove who a person is or what something is.

41.
absurd

Not making any sense; silly.

You think you saw a tiny green elephant under your bed? That's absurd!

[From the Latin word *absurdus,* "out of tune, not appropriate, absurd."]

WHAT THE OTHER WORDS MEAN

jovial: Full of fun and good cheer; jolly.

pertinent: Related to the matter being discussed or considered.

solemn: Very serious; grave.

42.

feline

Typical of cats.

*Purring is a feline trait,
shared by housecats and
lions.*

[From the Latin word *feles*, "cat."]

WHAT THE OTHER WORDS MEAN

bovine: Typical of cows or cattle.

canine: Typical of dogs.

equine: Typical of horses.

43.

panorama

A view of everything that can be seen over a wide area.

From the top floor of the skyscraper, you can see a panorama of the entire city.

[The painter Robert Barker (1739–1806) coined the word *panorama* by combining the Greek words *pan,* "all," and *horama,* "vision."]

WHAT THE OTHER WORDS MEAN

porthole: A small, usually round window in the side of a ship.

silhouette: A drawing consisting of an outline filled in with a solid color.

spectacle: An unusual or impressive happening, seen by many people, like fireworks.

One day in 1787, while sketching on top of a hill, the Scottish painter Robert Barker had an idea. What if he made a painting on the inside of a very large cylinder? People could stand inside the cylinder and see a complete landscape stretching away from them on all sides, no matter where they looked.

Barker coined the word **panorama** as a name for his new style of huge cylindrical paintings. He even constructed a special cylindrical building in London so that he could display his panoramas. The entrance fees made him rich.

Other artists imitated Barker, and panoramic paintings of famous views and battles became popular attractions in the United States, too. Eventually, the word *panorama* came to mean any broad view, not just a painted one.

upheaval

A lifting or upward movement of the earth's crust.

The upheaval that created the Appalachian Mountains occurred over 200 million years ago.

[From the English words *up* and *heave,* "to raise, to lift." The suffix *–al* at the end of *upheaval* shows that the word is a noun.]

WHAT THE OTHER WORDS MEAN

acceleration: An increase in speed.

instep: The arched middle part of the human foot.

valley: A long, narrow area of low land between mountains or hills.

droop

To bend or hang downward.

I could tell he was sleepy because his eyelids were drooping.

[From the medieval Norse word *drúpa*, "to droop, to hang one's head," related to the English words *drip* and *drop*.]

WHAT THE OTHER WORDS MEAN

drain: To cause something to become dry by allowing water to flow away.

dread: To be very scared of something.

drizzle: To rain in very fine drops.

46.

transport

To carry from one place to another.

A pail is useful for transporting water.

[From the Latin word *transportare*, "to carry over."]

WHAT THE OTHER WORDS MEAN

import: To bring in from another country for trade, sale, or use.

report: To give a spoken or written description of something.

support: To hold something in position or to keep it from falling.

integer

A positive or negative whole number or zero.

Numbers such as 5, 25, and –100 are integers. Numbers such as 1/3 and 2.5 are not integers.

[From the Latin word *integer*, "whole, complete."]

WHAT THE OTHER WORDS MEAN

fraction: Two numbers with a line between them that express a part of a whole.

infinity: A space, period of time, or quantity that has no limit.

ratio: A relationship in the amount, number, or size of two things.

A hole! What could make a hole right through a joist? What else but a rat, gnawing away all day? A rat at this moment out on his night prowl, a hungry rat who hadn't eaten for twenty-four hours—a pink-eyed, needle-toothed, **omnivorous**, giant rat?

—Lynne Reid Banks
The Indian in the Cupboard

omnivorous

Eating many kinds of food, including both meat and plants.

Grizzly bears are omnivorous. Their diet includes fish, insects, berries, and grasses.

[From the Latin word *omnivorus*, literally meaning "eating everything" and made by combining the Latin words *omnis*, "all," and *vorare*, "to swallow."]

WHAT THE OTHER WORDS MEAN

carnivorous: Eating the flesh of animals.

ravenous: Extremely hungry.

venomous: Producing or killing by means of poison, like spiders and some kinds of snakes.

pendulum

A weight hung, as in a clock, so that it can swing back and forth.

Because it is on a long cord, the pendulum swings very slowly.

[From Latin *pendulus*, "hanging."]

WHAT THE OTHER WORDS MEAN

equilibrium: Balance between opposite forces.

fulcrum: The point on which a lever turns when it is moving or lifting something.

spectrum: The bands of different colors that appear after light passes through a prism.

50.

passenger

A person riding in a car, airplane, or other vehicle.

The small sportscar can hold only one passenger.

[From the medieval French word *passageor*, "traveller," which comes from the medieval French word *passage*, "passage, travel."]

WHAT THE OTHER WORDS MEAN

participant: A person who takes part in something, such as a game.

pedestrian: A person traveling on foot.

spectator: A person who watches an event but does not take part in it.

urgent

Needing immediate attention.

This is an urgent situation: the baby has a high fever, and I must see the doctor right away.

[From the Latin word *urgere*, "to press, to urge." The English verb *to urge* is also from Latin *urgere*.]

WHAT THE OTHER WORDS MEAN

current: Belonging to the present time.

impressive: Creating a strong memory that stays in the mind for a long time; remarkable.

trite: Not interesting because of overuse or repetition.

akimbo

With the hands on the hips and the elbows bent outward.

The coach stood at the side of the field, arms akimbo, with a whistle in his mouth.

[From the medieval English expression *in kenebowe*, which may originally have meant "in jug-bows, like the handles of a jug." *Kenebowe* may be made up of the medieval French word *quenne*, "can, jug," and the medieval English word *bowe*, "something curved or bent, bow."]

WHAT THE OTHER WORDS MEAN

combo: Something that results from combining; a combination.

hobo: A person who wanders from place to place without a permanent home or steady job.

jumbo: Very large.

The last major pieces of construction in both castle and town defense were the gatehouses. Because these were the most **vulnerable** parts of the walls, they were designed and built with great care.

—David Macaulay
Castle

vulnerable

Easily harmed or attacked.

Small seedlings are especially vulnerable to frost.

[From the Latin word *vulnerare,* "to wound, to hurt."]

WHAT THE OTHER WORDS MEAN

abominable: Causing disgust or hatred.

durable: Capable of withstanding hard wear or long use.

tolerable: Capable of being endured or put up with.

54.

consecutive

Following one right after the other.

The team lost eight consec-utive games.

[From the Latin word *consequi,* "to follow closely."]

WHAT THE OTHER WORDS MEAN

affirmative: Saying that something is so, as with the word yes.

defective: Lacking a necessary part or quality; not perfect or complete.

diminutive: Very small; tiny.

insulate

To cover, surround, or line with a material that slows or prevents heat, electricity, or sound from passing through.

After we insulated the house, it stayed cooler in the summer and warmer in the winter.

[From the Latin word *insula*, "island," since an insulated object cannot be reached by something else, just as an island cannot be reached from the mainland without a boat.]

WHAT THE OTHER WORDS MEAN

gorge: To eat in a greedy way.

lubricate: To apply a slippery substance, such as grease or oil, to moving machine parts in order to reduce wear.

upholster: To fit furniture with stuffing, springs, and a fabric covering.

---

slogan

A word or phrase used by a business, team, or other group to advertise its aims or beliefs.

The new company slogan is designed to appeal to people who care about the environment.

[From the Scottish Gaelic and Irish word *sluagh-ghairm,* "war-cry." Scottish Gaelic and Irish, the Celtic languages of Scotland and Ireland, are closely related, and they share many words.]

WHAT THE OTHER WORDS MEAN

mascot: A person, animal, or object believed to bring good luck, especially one used as the symbol of a sports team.

notation: A system of symbols or figures used to represent things such as numbers or musical sounds.

refrain: A phrase or verse that is repeated regularly in a song or poem.

restrain

To prevent from doing something; hold back.

The barriers restrained the crowd from blocking the parade route.

[From the medieval French word *restraindre*, "to restrain."]

WHAT THE OTHER WORDS MEAN

relieve: To lessen or reduce pain or discomfort.

repeal: To do away with something, especially a law, officially or formally.

retire: To stop working at one's job, usually when one reaches a certain age.

58.

ukulele

A small guitar with four strings.

*A ukulele is easy to travel
with because it is so small.*

[From the Hawaiian word *ukulele*, "jumping
flea," made up of *uku*, "flea," and *lele*, "jumping."]

WHAT THE OTHER WORDS MEAN

accordion: A portable keyboard instrument in which air is forced
past reeds to create musical
sounds.

harp: A musical instrument made
up of a large triangular
frame on which a series of
strings are stretched.

xylophone: A musical instrument made
up of a row of wooden bars
of varying lengths that are
struck with small hammers
to make sounds.

Before Hawaii became part of the United States in 1898, it was an independent country ruled by kings and queens. King Kalakaua, who was king from 1874 to 1891, enjoyed music and dancing very much. In his court, a British man named Edward Purvis liked to entertain the king and the courtiers with his antics.

One day, Purvis heard someone playing a small, guitarlike instrument that local instrument makers had recently begun to make. He learned to play it, and his performances with it were an instant hit at the king's court. Even the king learned to play!

Since Purvis had a lively personality and was not very tall, the Hawaiians nicknamed him Ukulele. This means "jumping flea" in the native Hawaiian language. Eventually, **ukulele** became the word for Purvis's favorite instrument.

Define-α-Thon
Answer Key

1. improvise
2. plateau
3. universal
4. lazy
5. harmonize
6. petty
7. twitter
8. antenna
9. cryptic
10. tributary
11. sphinx
12. mandatory
13. admonish
14. opposite
15. quadruped
16. immunity
17. exempt
18. serenity
19. aquarium
20. opaque
21. toxic
22. agriculture
23. uncanny
24. irrigate
25. translate
26. geology
27. reservoir
28. uranium
29. atmosphere
30. manipulate
31. trudge
32. tranquil
33. monotonous
34. perimeter
35. reflex
36. amiable
37. cargo
38. pristine
39. tarpaulin
40. population
41. absurd
42. feline
43. panorama
44. upheaval
45. droop
46. transport
47. integer
48. omnivorous
49. pendulum
50. passenger
51. urgent
52. akimbo
53. vulnerable
54. consecutive
55. insulate
56. slogan
57. restrain
58. ukulele